Whole Food Plant-Based Air Fryer Cookbook

365 Days of Fast, Healthy Vegetarian Recipes You'll Want to Eat

Jelisia Clattery

CONTENTS

INTRODUCTION

Are you a plant-based dieter who wants to put this air fryer to better use? Then let me tell you some interesting ways to cook an all-vegan menu using nothing but your air fryer. Oil-free frying has made quite a buzz in the recent decade, and it has made people enjoy a variety of crispy meals without compromising on their health goals. In this cookbook, you will be getting a comprehensive collection of sixty plant-based recipes that you can try for breakfast, side meals, snacks, entrees, desserts and other types of meals. The best part about those recipes is that they are quick to make, and with the help of your air fry, you can get them ready with minimum effort.

CHAPTER 1: OVERVIEW

PLANT-BASED COOKING WITH THE AIR FRYER

First, let's make an understanding about what plant-based cooking is actually like? A plant-based diet basically excludes all meat, poultry, seafood, dairy, and eggs options from the menu, so as a cook, you are left with only plant-sourced food such as vegetables, fruits, grains, and legumes. You are left with a limited list of ingredients, but you can still add a variety of flavors to your menu using some creativity. What you really need to do is to create a menu by mixing and matching different plant-based ingredients, as you will find in the recipes given in this cookbook.

WHY THE PLANT-BASED DIET?

Plant-based foods are naturally high in vitamins, fibers and minerals, and they are cholesterol-free and have a low calorie and saturated fat content. Consuming a variety of these meals can offer our body all of the clean proteins, calcium, and other critical nutrients it requires. It's critical to get enough vitamin B12 from a healthy food source. A vitamin B12-enriched morning cereal, plant-based milk, and nutritional yeast can easily meet your vitamin B12 requirements. Eaters of a plant-based diet have a lower risk of heart disease, type 2 diabetes, obesity, and other diseases. A plant-based diet can also be less expensive than an omnivore one, according to research.

If you are new to the whole concept of a plant-based diet, then here are few simple techniques that will definitely help you get started with it successfully:

- Consume a lot of vegetables. At lunch and dinner, half your plate should be filled with veggies. When selecting vegetables, make sure to incorporate a variety of hues. Serve vegetables with hummus, salsa, or guacamole as a snack.

- Look for non-meat sources of proteins such as tofu, soybeans, tempeh, and seitan etc.

- Always choose healthy fats. Olives, Olive oil, nuts and nut butter, seeds, and avocados are all good sources of fat.

- Breakfast should include different grains. Oatmeal, quinoa, buckwheat, or barley are good places to start. Then toss in some nuts or seeds, as well as some fresh fruit.

- Every day, consume a variety of green leafy vegetables like kale, collards, Swiss chard, spinach, and other greens. To keep their flavour and nutrition, steam, grill, braise or stir-fry them.

- Make a salad the centrepiece of your meal. Salad greens, for instance, spinach, romaine, Bibb, or red leafy greens, should be added to the salads. Add a variety of different veggies, fresh herbs, beans, peas, or tofu to the mix.

The amazing thing about air fryers is that they work on a hot air mechanism with no use of oil. They are essentially small, powerful ovens as they use air as a heat source, whereas deep-frying uses hot oil as a heat source. As a result, air fryers are significantly less dirty and oil-intensive than deep-frying. Even better, these little ovens are capable of a lot more than just making fried food. Beautifully browned veggies, crackly-skinned chicken wings, and even light and fluffy pastries can all be cooked using an air fryer. Your air fryer functions much like a convection oven. It is small and compact in shape but powerful in function; it can roast, broil, or bake. It is not suitable for deep frying.

TIPS TO USE AN AIR FRYER

There are some common techniques and tips that help every beginner to use any air fryer with convenience without ending up with burnt or undercooked food:

- Keep the cooking grate in the basket at all times. This permits hot air to circulate around the dish while also preventing the food from becoming saturated with oil.
- It's a hands-on experience. Even browning necessitates removing the basket and toss or flipping the food every few minutes.
- It's alright to take a look through the basket. This can be done at any time during the cooking process. There's no need to turn off the machine because it turns off when the basket is removed.

- Make sure the drawer is fully closed before you resume frying, or it will not switch back on.
- The cooking time of air fryers is comparatively shorter than the ovens or other cooking appliances. So, it preheats quickly as well. So always keep an eye on the food and check it once it is cooked halfway through. Do not leave the food inside for too long.

MISTAKES TO AVOID DURING AIR FRYING

Some air fryer users complain that the food is cooked uneven or it doesn't turn out to be as crispy as expected or etc. little do, they know that most of such things result from some common mistakes we all commit at one point as a beginner, so they mistakes must be avoided:

Avoid being generous with the oil.

If you are going to use some oil to grease the food, then go easy on it! Excess oil collects in the drawer behind the grate, which may smoke upon heating. In general, if the meal already has fat on it, you may not need to add any amount of oil at all. If needed, only use lightly brush the oil to grease the ingredients.

Avoid Using low smoke point oils.

Such oil not only smokes at high temperatures in the air fryer but also leave an aftertaste in the food, which is unpleasant. The best oils to lightly grease the food for air frying include vegetable oil, canola oil, peanut oil, and other high smoke point oils.

Do not crowd the drawer.

Air fryers usually don't have a large capacity like an oven, as they are a compact countertop appliances. Don't overstuff the air fryer drawer or basket with food if you want your food to be cooked evenly. It's tempting to add all the food to the air fryer and cook everything at once, but it is not right. So always cook the food in batches.

Never forget to shake the basket.

Shaking the basket regularly during air frying ensures that the food is evenly heated, resulting in excellent browning. Shake the basket every five minutes, according to many recipes. Larger objects, such as breaded fish fillets should be flipped instead.

CHAPTER 2:

BREAKFASTS AND BRUNCHES

TOFU RANCHEROS

Preparation Time: 10 minutes

Cooking Time: 16 minutes

Serve: 4

Ingredients:

- 1 - 20 0z container Tofu, cut into cubes
- 1 teaspoon ground cumin powder
- 1 teaspoon ground chilli powder
- 1/2 teaspoon smoked paprika
- 1/4 teaspoon salt, or to taste

Salsa Beans:

- 1 (15.5 ounces) can black beans, drained
- 1/4 cup mild salsa
- 1/8 teaspoon liquid smoke
- 1/8 teaspoon jalapeno powder
- 1/8 teaspoon cumin powder
- Salt, to taste

Veggie Topping:

- 1/3 cup carrot, grated
- 1/3 cup zucchini, grated
- 1/3 cup yellow squash, grated
- 1/8 teaspoon salt

- 1 pinch black pepper

Base:

- 4 large flour tortillas
- 1 cup vegan cheese, shredded

Directions:

1. Mix tofu with salt, paprika, chilli powder and cumin in a bowl.
2. At 390 degrees F, preheat your Air fryer.
3. Add prepared tofu to the air fryer basket and air fry for 10 minutes.
4. Shake the tofu once cooked halfway through.
5. Mix all the ingredients for salsa beans in a suitable bowl.
6. Spread the tortillas in a flat pan and sear for 2-3 minutes per side.
7. Top each tortilla with ¼ vegan cheese, ¼ salsa beans, 14 tofu and shredded veggies.
8. Add a spoonful of mild salsa on top.
9. Serve.

Nutritional Value (Amount per Serving):

Calories 459; Fat 3.6g ; Cholesterol 0mg; Carbohydrate 82.5g; Sugars 3.8g; Protein 27.5g

Preparation Time: 15 minutes

Cooking Time: 10 minutes

Serve: 2

Ingredients:

Tofu:

- 8 oz. block of firm tofu, cut into 4 slices
- 1 teaspoon salt
- 1/2 teaspoon black pepper

Dry Ingredients:

- 1 1/2 cups all-purpose flour
- 1/3 cup cornstarch
- 1 tablespoon garlic powder
- 1 tablespoon onion powder
- 1 tablespoon salt
- 1 tablespoon paprika
- 2 teaspoon cayenne

Wet Ingredients:

- 1 cup soymilk
- 2 teaspoon apple cider vinegar
- 2 tablespoons Vegan Egg powder
- 1/2 cup ice-cold water
- 2 tablespoons bourbon
- 1 tablespoon hot sauce
- Spray oil

Directions:

1. At 400 degrees F, preheat your air fryer.
2. Mix bourbon with hot sauce, egg powder, water, vinegar and soy milk in a bowl.
3. Stir in flour, garlic powder and all the dry ingredients.
4. Mix well until smooth, then toss in tofu.
5. Place the coated tofu in the Air fryer basket and air fry for 10 minutes.
6. Flip the tofu once cooked halfway through.
7. Serve.

Nutritional Value (Amount per Serving):

Calories 297; Fat 2.8g; Cholesterol 0mg; Carbohydrate 54.4g; Sugars 4.1g; Protein 9.5g

Preparation Time: 10 minutes

Cooking Time: 6 minutes

Serve: 2

Ingredients:

- 1 regular gluten-free tortilla
- 2 tablespoons refried pinto beans
- 2 tablespoons grated vegan cheese
- 1 small corn tortilla
- 3 iceberg lettuce leaves
- 2 tablespoons guacamole
- 3 tablespoons salsa

Directions:

1. At 325 degrees F, preheat your Air fryer.
2. Spread the tortilla and top it with beans, cheese, salsa, corn and the rest of the ingredients.
3. Roll this tortilla neatly and place it in the air fryer basket.
4. Air fry this wrap for 6 minutes in the preheated air fryer.
5. Serve.

Nutritional Value (Amount per Serving):

Calories 264; Fat 13.9g; Cholesterol 0mg; Carbohydrate 29.5g; Sugars 1.7g; Protein 8g

TOFU SCRAMBLE

Preparation Time: 15 minutes

Cooking Time: 25 minutes

Serve: 2

Ingredients:

- 1 block tofu, chopped
- 2 tablespoons soy sauce
- 1 tablespoon olive oil
- 1 teaspoon turmeric
- ½ teaspoon garlic powder
- ½ teaspoon onion powder
- ½ cup chopped onion
- 2 ½ cups chopped red potato
- 1 tablespoon olive oil
- 4 cups broccoli florets

Directions:

1. At 400 degrees F, preheat your air fryer.
2. Mix tofu with onion, onion powder, garlic powder, turmeric, olive oil and soy sauce in a bowl.
3. Cover and marinate the tofu for 15 minutes.
4. Toss potatoes with olive oil and spread them in your air fryer basket.
5. Air fry the potatoes for 15 minutes in the preheated air fryer.
6. Add prepared tofu to the air fryer basket and air fry for 15 minutes; keep the marinade aside.
7. Toss the broccoli with the reserved marinade in a bowl.
8. Add broccoli to the air fryer basket and air fry for 5 minutes.
9. Serve.

Nutritional Value (Amount per Serving):

Calories 313; Fat 9.9g; Cholesterol 0mg; Carbohydrate 48.3g; Sugars 7.2g; Protein 14g

Preparation Time: 10 minutes

Cooking Time: 7 minutes

Serve: 4

Ingredients:

- 1 cup rolled oats
- 1 cup pecans
- 2 tablespoons ground flax seed
- 1 teaspoon ground cinnamon
- 8 pieces of whole-grain vegan bread
- ¾ cup almond milk
- Maple syrup, for serving

Directions:

1. At 350 degrees F, preheat your air fryer.
2. Add cinnamon, flaxseed, nuts and oats to a food processor and blend until crumbly.
3. Spread this mixture in a shallow pan.
4. Soak the bread in the milk for 15 seconds, then remove it.
5. Transfer the soaked bread to a baking pan suitable to fit the air fryer basket.
6. Spread the nutty mixture over the soaked bread.
7. Air fry the bread for 6 minutes in the preheated air fryer.
8. Serve with maple syrup on top.

Nutritional Value (Amount per Serving):

Calories 437; Fat 25.4g; Cholesterol 0mg; Carbohydrate 42.4g; Sugars 5.6g; Protein 12.9g

Preparation Time: 10 minutes

Cooking Time: 13 minutes

Serve: 2-4

Ingredients:

- 1 (20 ounces) can jackfruit, drained
- ⅓ cup Vegan Thousand Island Dressing
- 1 small sweet onion, peeled and diced
- 2 cloves garlic, peeled and minced
- 6 vegan cheese slices
- 2 dill pickles, chopped
- 12 vegan wonton wrappers

Directions:

1. Shred jackfruit with a fork and mix it with island dressing in a bowl.
2. Cover and marinate the jackfruit for 15 minutes.
3. Sauté garlic and onion with oil in a suitable saucepan for 5 minutes.
4. Remove this mixture from the heat and stir in the jackfruit mixture.
5. Spread a wonton wrapper in a diamond shape and add 2 tablespoons jackfruit mixture on the bottom corner.
6. Add ½ slice of cheese and 1 tablespoon pickles on top.
7. Roll the wrapper starting from the bottom.
8. Make more rolls in the same manner and brush each roll with pickle juice.
9. At 350 degrees F, preheat your Air fryer.
10. Place the rolls in the air fryer basket and air fry for 8 minutes.
11. Flip the rolls once cooked halfway through and resume cooking.
12. Serve warm.

Nutritional Value (Amount per Serving):

Calories 208; Fat 5.5g ; Cholesterol 14mg; Carbohydrate 38.9g; Sugars 0.7g; Protein 4.2g

Preparation Time: 10 minutes

Cooking Time: 19 minutes

Serve: 4

Ingredients:

- 1 cup raw cashew pieces
- ½ cup water
- 1 tablespoon nutritional yeast flakes
- ½ teaspoon white miso paste
- 1 small clove garlic, chopped
- ⅛ teaspoon salt
- 2 large Russet potatoes, sliced
- ½ teaspoon canola oil
- 1 pinch paprika
- 1 pinch pepper
- ¼ cup diced seitan bacon
- ¼ cup spring onions, sliced
- ¼ cup red onion, minced

Directions:

1. At 400 degrees F, preheat your air fryer.
2. Soak cashews in water in a bowl for 4 hours, then drain.
3. Blend cashews with 1/8 teaspoon salt, garlic, miso paste, nutritional yeast and ½ cup water in a blender until smooth.
4. Cut the potato into thick slices and place them in the air fryer basket.
5. Spray these slices with oil and drizzle black pepper, salt and paprika on top.
6. Air fry these potatoes for 10 minutes in the preheated air fryer.

7. Flip the potatoes and continue air frying for 4 minutes.

8. Sauté seitan bacon with ½ teaspoon oil in a skillet for 5 minutes.

9. Crumble the cooked seitan bacon once it is cooled.

10. Spread the cashew cream over air fried potato slices.

11. Add crumbled seitan and spring onions on top.

12. Serve.

Nutritional Value (Amount per Serving):

Calories 373; Fat 17.2g; Cholesterol 0mg; Carbohydrate 42.5g; Sugars 4.1g; Protein 15.2g

Preparation Time: 10 minutes

Cooking Time: 4 minutes

Serve: 4

Ingredients:

Marinated cashews:

- ½ cup raw cashew pieces
- 1 tablespoon olive oil
- 1 tablespoon lemon juice
- 1 teaspoon balsamic vinegar
- ½ teaspoon dried basil
- ½ teaspoon dried oregano
- ⅛ teaspoon granulated onion
- 1 garlic clove, minced
- Pinch salt

Crostini:

- 1 baguette cut into ½ inch slices
- Olive oil for toasting crostini
- 1 ½ cups hummus
- 1 cup grilled artichoke hearts from the oil-packed jar, drained and sliced

Directions:

1. Blend cashew with a pinch of salt, garlic, onion, oregano, basil, vinegar, oil and lemon juice in a blender until smooth.
2. At 380 degrees F, preheat your Air Fryer.

3.   Place the baguette slices in the Air fryer basket,

4.   Air fry them for 4 minutes in the preheated air fryer.

5.   Spread the hummus over the baguette slices.

6.   Divide the cashew mixture and grilled artichokes on top.

7.   Serve.

Nutritional Value (Amount per Serving):

Calories 273; Fat 14.9g; Cholesterol 0mg; Carbohydrate 28.7g; Sugars 1.5g; Protein 10.3g

Preparation Time: 10 minutes

Cooking Time: 16 minutes

Serve: 6

Ingredients:

Batter:

- ½ cup raw cashews
- 3 tablespoons almond milk
- ½ teaspoon hot sauce
- 1 tablespoon white miso paste
- 1 teaspoon mustard
- 16 ounces super firm tofu
- 6 tablespoons nutritional yeast flakes
- ½ teaspoon granulated onion
- ½ teaspoon paprika
- ½ teaspoon cumin
- ½ teaspoon ancho chilli powder
- ½ teaspoon salt
- ⅛ teaspoon turmeric
- ½ teaspoon canola oil

Add Ons:

- ½ cup seitan bacon
- ½ cup red bell pepper chopped small
- ½ cup onions chopped small
- ½ cup curly kale chopped

Directions:

1. Soak cashews in water overnight, then drain.
2. At 330 degrees F, preheat your air fryer.
3. Blend cashews with milk in a blender until smooth.
4. Stir in tofu and the rest of the ingredients, then blend until it makes a thick batter.
5. Fold in seitan bacon, pepper, onions, and kale, then mix well.
6. Divide the batter into a greased mini muffin cups.
7. Place the muffin cups in the Air fryer basket.
8. Air fry the quiches for 16 minutes in the preheated air fryer.
9. Serve.

Nutritional Value (Amount per Serving):

Calories 361; Fat 19g; Cholesterol 0mg; Carbohydrate 24.5g; Sugars 6.5g; Protein 25.5g

Preparation Time: 15 minutes

Cooking Time: 20 minutes

Serve: 2

Ingredients:

- 2 bagels, sliced
- 2 vegan breakfast sausages
- ½ teaspoon canola oil
- 4 super firm tofu, cut ¼ inch thick
- ¼ teaspoon salt
- ¼ teaspoon nutritional yeast flakes
- ¼ teaspoon granulated onion
- 1 pinch of black pepper
- 2 tablespoons vegan cream cheese

Directions:

1. At 400 degrees F, preheat your air fryer.
2. Cut the bagel in halves and toast them in a skillet until golden brown.
3. Place the breakfast vegan sausage in the air fryer basket.
4. Air fry the sausages for 10 minutes in the preheated air fryer.
5. Flip the vegan sausages once cooked halfway through.
6. Sear sliced tofu with oil in a skillet for 3-5 minutes per side.
7. Stir in salt, yeast, onion flakes, and black pepper.
8. Spread the cream cheese inside the bagels.
9. Add tofu to the bagels and serve.

Nutritional Value (Amount per Serving):

Calories 346; Fat 13.9g; Cholesterol 0mg; Carbohydrate 33.1g; Sugars 3.2g; Protein 20.9g

CHAPTER 3:

SNACKS AND SIDES

POPCORN TOFU NUGGETS

Preparation Time: 10 minutes

Cooking Time: 12 minutes

Serve: 2

Ingredients:

Popcorn Tofu

- 14 ounces tofu, drained and pressed
- ½ cup quinoa flour
- ½ cup cornmeal
- 3 tablespoons nutritional yeast
- 2 tablespoons Bouillon Vegetarian
- 1 tablespoon Dijon mustard
- 2 teaspoon garlic powder
- 2 teaspoon onion powder
- ½ teaspoon salt
- ½ teaspoon pepper
- ¾ cup almond milk
- 1.5 cup panko breadcrumbs

Directions:

1. At 350 degrees F, preheat your air fryer.
2. Mix flour with milk, pepper, salt, onion, garlic, mustard and bouillon in a bowl until smooth.

3. Dip the tofu in the batter and coat the panko breadcrumbs.

4. Place the coated tofu in the air fryer basket, then air fry for 12 minutes.

5. Flip the tofu nuggets once cooked halfway through.

6. Serve.

Nutritional Value (Amount per Serving):

Calories 392; Fat 8.7g; Cholesterol 0mg; Carbohydrate 59.3g; Sugars 5.1g; Protein 21.1g

Preparation Time: 10 minutes

Cooking Time: 15 minutes

Serve: 4

Ingredients:

- 3 yellow onions

Wet mix:

- 1/2 cup flour
- 2/3 cup almond milk
- 1/2 teaspoon paprika
- 1/4 teaspoon turmeric
- 1/2 teaspoon salt

Dry mix:

- 1 cup panko breadcrumbs
- 1/2 teaspoon paprika
- 1/4 teaspoon turmeric
- 1/4 teaspoon salt

Directions:

1. At 400 degrees F, preheat your Air fryer.
2. Mix flour with milk, paprika, turmeric, and salt in a bowl until smooth.
3. Toss breadcrumbs with salt, turmeric and paprika in a bowl.
4. Cut the onions into ½ inch thick slices and separate them into rings.
5. Dip each ring in the flour batter and coat with the panko crumbs.
6. Place the onion rings in the air fryer basket and air fry for 15 minutes.

7. Flip the onion rings once cooked halfway through, then resume cooking.

8. Serve and enjoy.

Nutritional Value (Amount per Serving):

Calories 139; Fat 1.4g; Cholesterol 0mg; Carbohydrate 27.1g; Sugars 4.2g; Protein 4.2g

Preparation Time: 10 minutes

Cooking Time: 15 minutes

Serve: 6

Ingredients:

- 1 15 ounces can chickpeas, drained
- 1 tablespoon sunflower oil
- 2 tablespoons lemon juice
- ¾ teaspoon smoked paprika
- ½ teaspoon ground cumin
- ½ teaspoon granulated garlic
- ¼ teaspoon granulated onion
- ½ teaspoon sea salt, more to taste
- ⅛ teaspoon cayenne pepper

Directions:

1. At 390 degrees F, preheat your air fryer.
2. Spread the rinsed chickpeas in the air fryer basket.
3. Mix oil with lemon juice, paprika, cumin, garlic, onion, salt and cayenne pepper in a bowl.
4. Spread this spice mixture over the chickpeas and toss well.
5. Air fry the chickpeas for 15 minutes in the preheated air fryer.
6. Toss the chickpeas after every 5 minutes.
7. Serve warm.

Nutritional Value (Amount per Serving):

Calories 107; Fat 4.4g; Cholesterol 0mg; Carbohydrate 14.3g; Sugars 0.3g; Protein 3.2g

KALE AND POTATO NUGGETS

Preparation Time: 10 minutes

Cooking Time: 19 minutes

Serve: 4

Ingredients:

- 2 cups chopped potatoes
- 1 teaspoon olive oil
- 1 clove garlic minced
- 4 cups chopped kale
- 1/8 cup almond milk
- 1/4 teaspoon sea salt
- 1/8 teaspoon ground black pepper
- Vegetable oil spray as needed

Directions:

1. Add potatoes to a saucepan filled with boiling water and cook for 30 minutes until soft.
2. Sauté garlic with oil in a skillet for 30 seconds until golden brown.
3. Stir in kale and cook for 3 minutes, then transfer it to a bowl.
4. Drain the cooked potatoes and allow them to cool.
5. Mash the cooked potatoes in a bowl with a potato masher.
6. Stir in kale, black pepper, milk, and salt, then mix well.
7. At 390 degrees F, preheat your Air fry.
8. Make 1-inch balls out of this potato mixture and place them in the air fryer basket.
9. Spray the potato nuggets with vegetable oil and air fry them for 15 minutes.
10. Flip the balls once cooked halfway through.

11. Serve.

Nutritional Value (Amount per Serving):

Calories 113; Fat 3g; Cholesterol 0mg; Carbohydrate 19.5g; Sugars 1.1g; Protein 3.5g

Preparation Time: 10 minutes

Cooking Time: 27 minutes

Serve: 4

Ingredients:

- 2 large sweet potatoes
- 2 tablespoons olive oil
- 2 tablespoons seasoning mix

Seasoning mix:

- 2 tablespoons ground coriander
- 1 tablespoon ground fennel
- 1 tablespoon dried oregano
- 1 tablespoon Aleppo Pepper
- 2 tablespoons kosher salt

Directions:

1. At 350 degrees F, preheat your Air fryer.
2. Mix coriander, fennel, oregano, Aleppo pepper and salt in a bowl.
3. Peel and cut the sweet potatoes in 1-inch-thick matchsticks.
4. Toss the sweet potatoes with olive oil and the seasoning mix.
5. Spread the sweet potatoes to the Air fryer basket.
6. Air fry these sweet potatoes fries for 27 minutes in the preheated air fryer.
7. Toss the fries after every 10 minutes.
8. Serve.

Nutritional Value (Amount per Serving):

Calories 157; Fat 7.5g; Cholesterol 0mg; Carbohydrate 22.4g; Sugars 0.4g; Protein 1.5g

Preparation Time: 10 minutes

Cooking Time: 30 minutes

Serve: 4

Ingredients:

- 3 medium red potatoes
- 1 teaspoon garlic powder
- 1 teaspoon onion powder
- ¼ teaspoon chilli powder
- ¼ teaspoon paprika
- ¼ teaspoon basil
- salt to taste

Directions:

1. At 400 degrees F, preheat your air fryer.
2. Peel, rinse and cut the potatoes into 1-inch matchsticks.
3. Toss the fries with garlic powder, onion powder, chilli powder, basil, paprika and salt in a bowl.
4. Spread the potato fries in the air fryer basket.
5. Air fry these fries for 30 minutes in the preheated air fryer.
6. Toss the fries after 15 minutes, then resume cooking.
7. Serve warm.

Nutritional Value (Amount per Serving):

Calories 117; Fat 0.3g; Cholesterol 0mg; Carbohydrate 26.6g; Sugars 2g; Protein 3.2g

Preparation Time: 10 minutes

Cooking Time: 15 minutes

Serve: 2

Ingredients:

- 1 large bunch kale, washed and torn
- 1 tablespoon olive oil
- 2 tablespoons za'atar seasoning
- 1 teaspoon sea salt

Directions:

1. Toss kale with olive oil and rub the leaves well.
2. Mix the leaves with salt and za'atar seasoning, then spread in the air fryer basket.
3. At 350 degrees F, preheat your air fryer.
4. Spread the kale leaves in the air fryer basket, and air fry them for 15 minutes.
5. Toss the kale leaves once cooked halfway through.
6. Serve.

Nutritional Value (Amount per Serving):

Calories 97; Fat 8g; Cholesterol 0mg; Carbohydrate 5.5g; Sugars 0g; Protein 2g

Preparation Time: 10 minutes

Cooking Time: 8 minutes

Serve: 4

Ingredients:

- ½ cup panko breadcrumbs
- 2 teaspoon nutritional yeast flakes
- 1 teaspoon dried basil
- 1 teaspoon dried oregano
- 1 teaspoon garlic powder
- Pinch salt and black pepper
- ¼ cup aquafaba liquid
- 8 ounces thawed vegan ravioli
- Spritz cooking spray

Directions:

1. At 390 degrees F, preheat your air fryer.
2. Mix panko crumbs with salt, black pepper, garlic powder, oregano, basil and yeast on a plate.
3. Add aquafaba to a bowl and dip the ravioli in this liquid.
4. Coat the ravioli with the panko crumbs mixture.
5. Place the coated ravioli in the air fryer basket.
6. Spray the ravioli with cooking spray and air fry for 8 minutes.
7. Flip the ravioli once cooked halfway through.
8. Serve warm.

Nutritional Value (Amount per Serving):

Calories 120; Fat 1g; Cholesterol 0mg; Carbohydrate 23g; Sugars 1.5g; Protein 4.7g

Preparation Time: 15 minutes

Cooking Time: 8 minutes

Serve: 2

Ingredients:

- 1 cup warm water
- 1 teaspoon vegetarian Bouillon
- 1 cup soy curls
- ¼ cup BBQ sauce
- 1 teaspoon canola oil

Directions:

1. Mix water with bouillon in a large bowl.
2. Soak soy curls in this water for 10 minutes, then drain.
3. At 400 degrees F, preheat your air fryer.
4. Pull the curls to shred them into finer strips.
5. Spread the soy curls in the air fryer basket and air fry for 3 minutes.
6. Mix the soy curls with ¼ cup of bbq sauce in a bowl.
7. Return these curls to the air fryer basket and air fry for 5 minutes.
8. Serve warm.

Nutritional Value (Amount per Serving):

Calories 117; Fat 4.7g; Cholesterol 0mg; Carbohydrate 13.8g; Sugars 8.6g; Protein 5g

Preparation Time: 10 minutes

Cooking Time: 18 minutes

Serve: 4

Ingredients:

- 2 cups cauliflower florets
- 1 cup panko breadcrumbs

Buffalo Coating:

- ¼ cup melted vegan butter
- ¼ cup vegan Buffalo sauce

Directions:

1. At 350 degrees F, preheat your air fryer.
2. Melt the vegan butter in a bowl by heating it in the microwave for 30 seconds.
3. Stir in buffalo sauce and mix well.
4. Dip the cauliflower florets in the buffalo sauce mixture and then coat them with breadcrumbs.
5. Spread the coated florets in the air fryer basket.
6. Air fry the buffalo cauliflower florets for 17 minutes.
7. Flip the florets once cooked halfway through.
8. Serve warm.

Nutritional Value (Amount per Serving):

Calories 190; Fat 2.2g; Cholesterol 0mg; Carbohydrate 37.7g; Sugars 3.5g; Protein 6.4g

CHAPTER 4:

SALADS AND HANDHELDS

TOFU WITH THAI SLAW

Preparation Time: 15 minutes

Cooking Time: 10 minutes

Serve: 4

Ingredients:

- 1 (16-oz) block extra-firm tofu, cubed
- Salt, to taste
- 1 tablespoon olive oil
- Black pepper, to taste

Salad:

- ¼ cup cashew butter
- 2 tablespoons white miso paste
- 2 tablespoons lime juice
- 1 teaspoon sesame oil
- 1 teaspoon grated ginger
- 5 tablespoons water
- 7 cups red cabbage, shredded
- 2 scallions, chopped
- ½ cup cilantro, chopped
- ½ cup fresh basil
- 2 Thai chiles pepper, diced
- Salt, to taste
- ¼ cup toasted peanuts

Directions:

1. At 400 degrees F, preheat your Air Fryer.
2. Toss tofu with black pepper, salt and oil in a bowl.
3. Spread the tofu cubes in the Air Fryer basket.
4. Air fry them for 10 minutes and shake once cooked halfway through.
5. Meanwhile, toss all the salad ingredients in a suitable salad bowl.
6. Mix well and top the salad with tofu cubes.
7. Serve fresh.

Nutritional Values:

Calories 195; Fat 13.8g; Cholesterol 0mg; Carbohydrate 14.8g; Sugars 4.5g; Protein 6.9g

Preparation Time: 15 minutes

Cooking Time: 10 minutes

Serve: 4

Ingredients:

- 1-pound broccoli crowns
- 1 (16-oz) block extra-firm tofu, cubed
- Salt, to taste
- 1 tablespoon olive oil
- Black pepper, to taste

Salad:

- 3 tablespoons olive oil
- 3 tablespoons mayo
- 1½ tablespoons apple cider vinegar
- 2 teaspoon Dijon mustard
- 1 teaspoon choc zero maple syrup
- 1 garlic clove, minced
- ⅓ cup diced red onions
- ⅓ cup dried cranberries

Directions:

1. At 350 degrees F, preheat your Air Fryer.
2. Toss tofu with broccoli, black pepper, salt and oil in a bowl.
3. Spread the tofu cubes in the Air Fryer basket.
4. Air fry them for 10 minutes and shake once cooked halfway through.
5. Meanwhile, toss all the salad ingredients in a suitable salad bowl.
6. Mix well and toss in tofu and broccoli.

7. Serve fresh.

Nutritional Values:

Calories 157; Fat 9g; Cholesterol 3mg; Carbohydrate 13.6g; Sugars 1.8g; Protein 6.7g

Preparation Time: 15 minutes

Cooking Time: 7 minutes

Serve: 4

Ingredients:

- 4 cups Brussels sprouts
- 1 onion, shredded
- ¼ cup olive oil
- ¼ cup fresh lemon juice
- ½ cup pine nuts, toasted
- ⅓ cup dried cranberries
- ⅓ cup chopped chives
- Salt and black pepper, to taste

Directions:

1. At 400 degrees F, preheat your Air Fryer.
2. Toss Brussel sprouts with 2 tablespoons oil in a bowl.
3. Spread the Brussel sprouts in the Air Fryer basket.
4. Air fry them for 7 minutes and shake once cooked halfway through.
5. Meanwhile, toss all the salad ingredients in a suitable salad bowl.
6. Mix well and top the salad with tofu cubes.
7. Serve fresh.

Nutritional Values:

Calories 281; Fat 24.7g; Cholesterol 0mg; Carbohydrate 14.1g; Sugars 4.4g; Protein 5.9g

Preparation Time: 15 minutes

Cooking Time: 10 minutes

Serve: 4

Ingredients:

- 1 (16-oz) block extra-firm tofu, cubed
- Salt, to taste
- 1 tablespoon olive oil
- Black pepper, to taste

Salad:

- ¼ teaspoon salt
- 1 big bunch curly green kale, chopped
- ½ cup raw sliced almonds
- ⅓ cup dried cherries, chopped
- 4 oz. vegan feta cheese, crumbled

Vinaigrette:

- ⅓ cup olive oil
- 1 tablespoon sherry vinegar
- 1 tablespoon Dijon mustard
- 2 garlic cloves, minced
- ¼ teaspoon salt

Directions:

1. At 400 degrees F, preheat your Air Fryer.
2. Toss tofu with black pepper, salt and oil in a bowl.
3. Spread the tofu cubes in the Air Fryer basket.

4. Air fry them for 10 minutes and shake once cooked halfway through.

5. Meanwhile, toss all the salad ingredients in a suitable salad bowl.

6. Mix well and top the salad with tofu cubes.

7. Serve fresh.

8. Enjoy.

Nutritional Values:

Calories 262; Fat 27.3g; Cholesterol 0mg; Carbohydrate 3.6g; Sugars 0.7g; Protein 4.4g

Preparation Time: 15 minutes

Cooking Time: 10 minutes

Serve: 2

Ingredients:

- 4 medium zucchini, peeled and sliced
- 2 tbsp. olive oil
- 2 tbsp. lemon juice
- 2 small garlic cloves, chopped
- 2 tbsp. parsley, chopped
- ¼ tsp. salt

Directions:

1. At 400 degrees F, preheat your Air Fryer.
2. Toss zucchini with lemon juice, garlic, salt and oil in a bowl.
3. Spread the zucchini in the Air Fryer basket.
4. Air fry them for 10 minutes and shake once cooked halfway through.
5. Add parsley on top and mix well.
6. Serve fresh.

Nutritional Values:

Calories 192; Fat 14.9g; Cholesterol 0mg; Carbohydrate 14.7g; Sugars 7.2g; Protein 5.2g

Preparation Time: 15 minutes

Cooking Time: 11 minutes

Serve: 4

Ingredients:

- 1½ cups cherry tomatoes, sliced in half
- 3-4 small eggplant, sliced
- Olive oil for drizzling
- 1 garlic clove, minced
- ½ cup pine nuts, toasted
- 1 handful of arugulas
- 1 handful of torn basil
- Generous splashes of sherry vinegar
- Salt and black pepper, to taste

Directions:

1. At 400 degrees F, preheat your Air Fryer.
2. Toss eggplant with oil in a bowl.
3. Spread the eggplant in the Air Fryer basket.
4. Air fry them for 11 minutes and shake once cooked halfway through.
5. Meanwhile, toss all the salad ingredients in a suitable salad bowl.
6. Mix well and top the salad with eggplant.
7. Serve fresh.

Nutritional Values:

Calories 267; Fat 2.3g; Cholesterol 0mg; Carbohydrate 60.7g; Sugars 34g; Protein 11.6g

Preparation Time: 10 minutes

Cooking Time: 10 minutes

Serve: 4

Ingredients:

- 1 large cauliflower head, cut into florets
- 2 tbsp olive oil
- 1/2 tsp salt
- 1/2 tsp black pepper

Salad:

- 1 celery stalk, sliced
- 1/3 cup hazelnuts, raw, skin on
- 1/2 pomegranate, seeds only
- 1 cup parsley leaves, chopped

Dressing:

- 2 tbsp olive oil
- 1/3 tsp cinnamon powder
- 1/3 tsp allspice
- 1 tbsp sherry vinegar
- 1 1/2 tsp maple syrup
- 1/4 tsp salt
- 1/4 tsp black pepper

Directions:

1. At 400 degrees F, preheat your Air Fryer.
2. Toss cauliflower florets with black pepper, salt and oil in a bowl.

3. Spread cauliflower florets in the Air Fryer basket.

4. Air fry them for 10 minutes and shake once cooked halfway through.

5. Meanwhile, toss all the salad and dressing ingredients in a suitable salad bowl.

6. Mix well and toss in air fried cauliflower florets then mix well.

7. Serve fresh.

Nutritional Values:

Calories 178; Fat 11.2g; Cholesterol 0mg; Carbohydrate 18.5g; Sugars 9.6g; Protein 5.7g

Preparation Time: 15 minutes

Cooking Time: 8 minutes

Serve: 4

Ingredients:

- 1 bunch of curly green kale
- 12 Brussels sprouts
- ¼ cup sliced almonds
- ¼ cup shaved vegan Parmesan
- Salt, to taste

Tahini-maple dressing:

- ¼ cup tahini
- 2 tablespoons white wine vinegar
- 2 teaspoon white miso
- 2 teaspoon choc zero maple syrup
- Pinch of red pepper flakes
- ¼ cup water

Directions:

1. At 400 degrees F, preheat your Air Fryer.
2. Toss brussels sprouts with salt in a bowl.
3. Spread the brussels sprouts in the Air Fryer basket.
4. Air fry them for 8 minutes and shake once cooked halfway through.
5. Meanwhile, toss all the salad ingredients in a suitable salad bowl.
6. Mix well and stir in brussels sprouts.
7. Serve fresh.

Nutritional Values:

Calories 221; Fat 14.6g; Cholesterol 10mg; Carbohydrate 15g; Sugars 1.8g; Protein 12.1g

Preparation Time: 5 minutes

Cooking Time: 6 minutes

Serve: 6

Ingredients:

- 2 heads of broccoli, cut into florets
- 2 teaspoons olive oil
- 1/2 teaspoon salt
- 1/2 cup almonds
- 1/4 cup dried cranberries
- 1 tablespoon fresh dill, chopped
- 4 very thin slices of lemon

Lemony Dressing:

- 1/4 cup lemon juice
- 1 tablespoon maple syrup
- 1 teaspoon Dijon mustard
- 1 teaspoon balsamic vinegar
- 1 garlic clove, grated
- 2 tablespoons olive oil

Directions:

1. At 350 degrees F, preheat your Air Fryer.
2. Toss broccoli florets with oil and salt in the Air Fryer basket.
3. Air fry them for 6 minutes in the air fryer basket.
4. Mix lemon juice, maple syrup, Dijon mustard, vinegar, garlic and olive oil in a salad bowl.
5. Toss in broccoli, almond, dill, cranberries and lemon slices.

6. Mix well and serve.

Nutritional Values:

Calories 203; Fat 10.3g; Cholesterol 0mg; Carbohydrate 25.9g; Sugars 12.9g; Protein 7.6g

Preparation Time: 5 minutes

Cooking Time: 10 minutes

Serve: 4

Ingredients:

- 1 (16-oz) block tempeh, diced
- Salt, to taste
- 1 tablespoon olive oil
- Black pepper, to taste

Salad:

- 4 ripe tomatoes, cubed
- 4 oz. vegan mozzarella cheese, cubed
- 2 avocados, peeled, pitted, and cubed
- 3 tablespoons balsamic vinegar
- 3 tablespoons red wine vinegar
- ½ teaspoon dried basil
- salt and ground black pepper to taste

Directions:

1. At 370 degrees F, preheat your Air Fryer.
2. Toss tempeh with black pepper, salt and oil in a bowl.
3. Spread the tempeh cubes in the Air Fryer basket.
4. Air fry them for 10 minutes and shake once cooked halfway through.
5. Meanwhile, toss all the salad ingredients in a suitable salad bowl.
6. Mix well and top the salad with tempeh cubes.
7. Serve fresh.

Nutritional Values:

Calories 303; Fat 23.9g; Cholesterol 0mg; Carbohydrate 18.6g; Sugars 2.5g;
Protein 12.6g

CHAPTER 5:

MAIN DISHES

ARTICHOKE HEARTS WITH GARLIC AIOLI

Preparation Time: 15 minutes

Cooking Time: 8 minutes

Serve: 6

Ingredients:

Artichoke hearts:

- 14 water-packed artichoke hearts
- 1/2 cup almond flour
- 1/4 teaspoon baking powder
- 1 pinch salt
- 8 tablespoons water
- 6 tablespoons almond meal
- 1/4 teaspoon dried basil
- 1/4 teaspoon dried oregano
- 1/4 teaspoon paprika
- 1/4 teaspoon granulated garlic
- Spritz canola oil

Lemon garlic aioli:

- 3/4 cup mayonnaise
- 1 garlic clove minced
- 1 teaspoon lemon juice

- 1/8 teaspoon granulated onion
- Pinch salt

Directions:

1. Drain the artichokes and toss with the rest of the ingredients in a bowl.
2. Spread the artichokes in the Air Fryer basket.
3. Return the basket to the Air Fryer.
4. Air fry them for 8 minutes and flip once cooked halfway through.
5. Mix all the garlic aioli ingredients in a bowl.
6. Serve the artichokes with garlic aioli.

Nutritional Values:

Calories 343; Fat 14.5g; Cholesterol 8mg; Carbohydrate 49g; Sugars 5.9g; Protein 14.5g

Preparation Time: 10 minutes

Cooking Time: 9 minutes

Serve: 4

Ingredients:

- 4 tablespoons unsalted butter
- 3 garlic cloves, minced
- 1 1/2 tablespoons soy sauce
- 36 cremini mushrooms with 2-inch caps
- 2 teaspoon fresh thyme leaves, chopped
- Salt

Directions:

1. Toss mushrooms with soy sauce, butter, garlic, thyme and salt in a bowl.
2. Thread these mushrooms on the wooden skewers.
3. Place the seasoned mushroom skewers in the Air Fryer basket.
4. Return the basket to the Air Fryer.
5. Air fry them for 9 minutes and flip once cooked halfway through. Serve warm.

Nutritional Values:

Calories 290; Fat 11.6g; Cholesterol 31mg; Carbohydrate 28.5g; Sugars 9.1g; Protein 18.7g

Preparation Time: 10 minutes

Cooking Time: 13 minutes

Serve: 2

Ingredients:

- 4 cups medium-sized cauliflower florets
- 1 teaspoon canola oil
- Pinch salt
- 2 teaspoon lemon juice
- 1/8 teaspoon sumac

Directions:

1. At 400 degrees F, preheat your Air Fryer.
2. Toss cauliflower with lemon and the rest of the ingredients in a bowl.
3. Spread the cauliflower in the Air Fryer basket.
4. Return the Air Fryer basket to the Air Fryer.
5. Air fry the cauliflower for 13 minutes.
6. Shake them once cooked halfway through. Serve.

Nutritional Values:

Calories 62; Fat 2.4g; Cholesterol 0mg; Carbohydrate 8.1g; Sugars 2.1g;
Protein 2g

Preparation Time: 10 minutes

Cooking Time: 10 minutes

Serve: 2

Ingredients:

- 1/2 cup almond meal
- 3 tablespoons xanthan gum
- 1/4 cup mayonnaise
- 1/2 teaspoon dried basil
- 1/2 teaspoon dried oregano
- 1/2 teaspoon granulated onion
- Salt and black pepper, to taste
- 1 medium-sized green tomato, sliced
- Spritz oil spray

Directions:

1. Mix mayonnaise, basil, oregano, onion, black pepper, salt, and xanthan gum in a bowl.
2. Di the green tomatoes slices in the mayo mixture.
3. Coat them with almond meal.
4. Place these slices in the Air Fryer basket.
5. Return the basket to the Air Fryer.
6. Air fry them for 10 minutes and flip once cooked halfway through.
7. Serve warm.

Nutritional Values:

Calories 267; Fat 21.9g; Cholesterol 8mg; Carbohydrate 15.5g; Sugars 5.4g; Protein 6.1g

Preparation Time: 10 minutes

Cooking Time: 10 minutes

Serve: 4

Ingredients:

- 1-pint whole mushrooms, portabella
- 1 green pepper, deseeded and diced
- 1 yellow pepper, deseeded and diced
- 1 onion, cut into 2-inch pieces
- 1-pint grape tomatoes

Marinade:

- 1/4 cup olive oil
- 2 garlic cloves, minced
- Juice of 1 lemon
- 1/2 teaspoon dried oregano
- 1/2 teaspoon salt

Directions:

1. At 400 degrees F, preheat your Air Fryer.
2. Toss mushrooms with bell pepper and the rest of the ingredients in a bowl.
3. Thread these mushrooms and veggies on the wooden skewers.
4. Place the vegetable skewers in the Air Fryer basket.
5. Return the basket to the Air Fryer.
6. Air fry them for 10 minutes and flip once cooked halfway through.
7. Serve warm.

Nutritional Values:

Calories 164; Fat 13.1g; Cholesterol 0mg; Carbohydrate 12.2g; Sugars 4.9g; Protein 3g

Preparation Time: 10 minutes

Cooking Time: 10 minutes

Serve: 4

Ingredients:

- 1 large cauliflower head, cut into steaks
- Salt and black pepper, to taste

Dry ingredients:

- 1 1/2 cups almond flour
- 1/3 cup xanthan gum
- 1 tablespoon garlic powder
- 1 tablespoon onion powder
- 1 tablespoon salt
- 1 tablespoon paprika
- 2 teaspoon cayenne

Wet ingredients:

- 1 cup soymilk
- 2 teaspoon apple cider vinegar
- 2 tablespoons vegan egg powder
- 1/2 cup ice-cold water
- 2 tablespoons bourbon
- 1 tablespoon hot sauce

Directions:

1. Mix soy milk with all the wet and dry ingredients in a bowl.
2. Dip the cauliflower in the flour batter
3. At 400 degrees F, preheat your Air Fryer.
4. Spread the cauliflower in the Air Fryer basket.

5. Return the Air Fryer basket to the Air Fryer.

6. Air fry the cauliflower for 10 minutes.

7. Shake them once cooked halfway through. Serve.

Nutritional Values:

Calories 230; Fat 5.4g; Cholesterol 38mg; Carbohydrate 39.6g; Sugars 13.4g; Protein 15g

Preparation Time: 10 minutes

Cooking Time: 10 minutes

Serve: 4

Ingredients:

- 14 oz. tofu
- 2 tablespoons sesame oil
- 1/4 cup soy sauce
- ¼ cup edamame beans
- 3 tablespoons maple syrup
- 2 tablespoons lime juice
- 1 tablespoon Sriracha
- 1 lb. fresh broccoli florets only
- 3 medium carrots peeled and sliced
- 1 red bell pepper sliced
- 8 oz. fresh spinach sautéed

Directions:

1. Mix tofu with sesame oil, sriracha, soy sauce and lime juice in a bowl.
2. Spread the tofu in the Air Fryer basket.
3. Air fry them for 10 minutes at 400 degrees F.
4. Toss them once cooked halfway through.
5. Mix broccoli, carrots, edamame beans, bell pepper and spinach in a bowl.
6. Top them with air fried tofu.
7. Enjoy.

Nutritional Values:

Calories 230; Fat 11.5g; Cholesterol 0mg; Carbohydrate 24.2g; Sugars 11.6g; Protein 13.3g

Preparation Time: 10 minutes

Cooking Time: 12 minutes

Serve: 4

Ingredients:

- 3 cups broccoli florets
- 3 cups cauliflower florets
- 2 tablespoons olive oil
- ½ teaspoon garlic powder
- ¼ teaspoon salt
- ¼ teaspoon paprika
- ⅛ teaspoon ground black pepper

Directions:

1. At 400 degrees F, preheat your Air Fryer.
2. Toss cauliflower with broccoli and the rest of the ingredients in a bowl.
3. Spread the cauliflower mixture in the Air Fryer basket.
4. Return the Air Fryer basket to the Air Fryer.
5. Air fry the cauliflower for 12 minutes.
6. Shake them once cooked halfway through.
7. Serve.

Nutritional Values:

Calories 207; Fat 14.6g; Cholesterol 0mg; Carbohydrate 17.7g; Sugars 6.1g; Protein 7g

Preparation Time: 10 minutes

Cooking Time: 15 minutes

Serve: 4

Ingredients:

- 1 cup mushrooms, sliced
- 1 red bell pepper sliced into ½ inch slices
- 1 yellow bell pepper sliced into ½ inch slices
- 1 green bell pepper sliced into ½ inch slices
- 1 red onion sliced into wedges
- 3 tablespoons fajita seasoning
- 1 tablespoon vegetable oil

Directions:

1. At 390 degrees F, preheat your Air Fryer.
2. Toss mushrooms with peppers, onion fajita seasoning and oil in a bowl.
3. Spread the fajita mixture in the Air Fryer basket.
4. Spray them with cooking spray.
5. Return the Air Fryer basket to the Air Fryer.
6. Air fry these veggies for 15 minutes.
7. Serve warm.

Nutritional Values:

Calories 255; Fat 13.8g; Cholesterol 0mg; Carbohydrate 27.2g; Sugars 5.2g; Protein 3.2g

Preparation Time: 10 minutes

Cooking Time: 10 minutes

Serve: 2

Ingredients:

- 2 bell peppers, diced
- 1 eggplant, diced
- 1 zucchini, diced
- 1/2 onion, diced
- salt and black pepper, to taste

Directions:

1. At 390 degrees F, preheat your Air Fryer.
2. Thread bell peppers, eggplant, zucchini, and onion on wooden skewers, alternately.
3. Spread the skewers in the Air Fryer basket.
4. Spray them with cooking spray and seasoning with black pepper and salt.
5. Return the Air Fryer basket to the Air Fryer.
6. Air fry these skewers for 10 minutes. Serve warm.

Nutritional Values:

Calories 312; Fat 1.9g; Cholesterol 0mg; Carbohydrate 28.3g; Sugars 15.7g; Protein 4.9g

CHAPTER 6:

DESSERTS

APPLE HAND PIES

Preparation Time: 15 minutes

Cooking Time: 10 minutes

Serve: 6

Ingredients:

- 14 ounces refrigerated package pie crust (2 crusts)
- 1/2 (21 ounces) can apple pie filling
- 2 tablespoons almond butter
- 3 teaspoon turbinado sugar
- Caramel sauce for dipping

Directions:

1. At 350 degrees F, preheat your air fryer.
2. Spread the pie crusts on the working surface.
3. Cut 5-inch circles out of the crusts using a cookie cutter.
4. Add two slices of apples from the pie filling at the center of each round.
5. Fold the dough circles in half and press edges with a fork to seal the filling.
6. Place the apple hand pies in the air fryer basket.
7. Brush the almond butter over the handpieces and drizzle sugar on top.
8. Cut three slits on top of each hand pie and air fry for 10 minutes.
9. Serve with caramel sauce.

Nutritional Value (Amount per Serving):

Calories 349; Fat 13.2g; Cholesterol 5mg; Carbohydrate 56.7g; Sugars 26.4g; Protein 4.6g

Preparation Time: 10 minutes

Cooking Time: 12 minutes

Serve: 6

Ingredients:

- 1 cup self-rising flour
- 1 cup soy yogurt
- 2 tablespoons sugar
- 1 teaspoon vanilla
- 2 tablespoons melted almond butter
- 1/2 cup powdered sugar

Directions:

1. Mix yogurt, sugar and vanilla in a mixing bowl.
2. Stir in flour and mix until it makes a smooth dough.
3. Knead the dough for 5 minutes, then spread into a 1inch thick rectangle.
4. Cut this dough into 9 equal pieces and dust each piece with some flour.
5. Leave these dough pieces for 15 minutes.
6. At 350 degrees F, preheat your air fryer.
7. Grease the air fryer basket with cooking oil spray.
8. Transfer the prepared dough pieces to the basket and brush them with melted butter.
9. Air fry the beignets for 12 minutes until golden brown.
10. Flip the beignets once cooked halfway through.
11. Dust the beignets with powdered sugar.
12. Serve.

Nutritional Value (Amount per Serving):

Calories 294; Fat 6.1g; Cholesterol 0mg; Carbohydrate 52.7g; Sugars 25.7g; Protein 7.7g

Preparation Time: 15 minutes

Cooking Time: 15 minutes

Serve: 4

Ingredients:

- 2 apples
- 1 teaspoon almond butter, melted
- ½ teaspoon cinnamon

Topping:

- ⅓ cup old fashioned oats
- 1 tablespoon almond butter, melted
- 1 tablespoon maple syrup
- 1 teaspoon whole meal flour
- ½ teaspoon cinnamon

Directions:

1. At 350 degrees F, preheat your air fryer.
2. Cut the whole apples in half crosswise and remove the core using a knife.
3. Brush the apples with butter and spring cinnamon over them.
4. Mix oats with butter, maple syrup, cinnamon and a whole meal in a bowl.
5. Stuff the apples with the oats mixture and place them in the air fryer basket.
6. Air fry these apples for 15 minutes in the preheated air fryer.
7. Serve once cooled.

Nutritional Value (Amount per Serving):

Calories 168; Fat 3.5g; Cholesterol 0mg; Carbohydrate 32.5g; Sugars 15.1g; Protein 3.6g

Preparation Time: 10 minutes

Cooking Time: 10 minutes

Serve: 6

Ingredients:

- 2 cups bread cubed
- 2/3 cup coconut cream
- 1/2 teaspoon vanilla extract
- 1/4 cup sugar
- 1/4 cup chocolate chips

Directions:

1. At 350 degrees F, preheat your air fryer.
2. Grease a baking dish suitable for your air fryer with cooking spray.
3. Spread the bread cubes in the baking dish.
4. Add chocolate chips on top of the bread cubes.
5. Beat cream with vanilla extract and sugar in a bowl.
6. Spread the cream mixture over the bread cubes.
7. Air fry the pudding for 10 minutes in the air fryer.

Nutritional Value (Amount per Serving):

Calories 154; Fat 8.8g; Cholesterol 2mg; Carbohydrate 17.9g; Sugars 13.4g; Protein 2.4g

Preparation Time: 10 minutes

Cooking Time: 12 minutes

Serve: 8

Ingredients:

- 1 box store-bought pie crust
- 1/2 cup berry jam
- 1/2 cup berries
- ¼ cup almond butter, melted
- 2 tablespoons caster sugar

Directions:

1. At 375 degrees F, preheat your air fryer.
2. Roll out the pie crusts and cut 14 (4 inches) circles out of this dough using a cookie cutter.
3. Knead the leftover dough and roll out again to cut 2 more circles.
4. Add 2 tablespoons of berry jam at the center of 8 dough circles.
5. Place the remaining dough circles on top and press the edges with a fork to seal them.
6. Brush the hand pies with almond butter and drizzle sugar on top.
7. Place the berry hand pies in the air fryer basket and air fry for 12 minutes.
8. Flip the hand pies once cooked halfway through.
9. Serve.

Nutritional Value (Amount per Serving):

Calories 167; Fat 7.3g; Cholesterol 0mg; Carbohydrate 25.3g; Sugars 13.8g; Protein 1.1g

Preparation Time: 15 minutes

Cooking Time: 10 minutes

Serve: 8

Ingredients:

- 1 (8 ounces) can vegan cream cheese, softened
- 1/4 cup coconut cream
- 1-1/2 tablespoons granulated sugar
- 1 teaspoon vanilla extract
- 8 medium strawberries, quartered
- 1 medium banana, peeled and sliced
- 8 soft flour tortillas
- 8 teaspoons Nutella
- olive oil spray

Directions:

1. Mix sugar, vegan cream cheese, sugar and coconut cream in a bowl.
2. Divide the vegan cream cheese mixture into two bowls.
3. Add strawberries to one bowl and sliced bananas to another bowl.
4. Spread a tortilla on the working surface.
5. Add ¼ of the strawberry mixture to the left of the center of the tortilla.
6. Add a teaspoon of Nutella on the side and roll the tortilla like a burrito.
7. Repeat the same steps with the remaining strawberry and banana filling and tortillas.
8. At 350 degrees F, preheat your air fryer.
9. Place the rolled chimichangas in the air fryer basket.
10. Spray them with cooking oil and the air fryer for 10 minutes.
11. Flip the rolls once cooked halfway through.

12. Serve.

Nutritional Value (Amount per Serving):

Calories 299; Fat 17g; Cholesterol 0mg; Carbohydrate 32.7g; Sugars 10g; Protein 5g

Preparation Time: 15 minutes

Cooking Time: 15 minutes

Serve: 6

Ingredients:

- 1 cup 2 tablespoons all-purpose flour
- ½ teaspoon baking soda
- ½ teaspoon salt
- 6 tablespoons almond butter
- ⅓ cup granulated sugar
- ¼ cup light brown sugar
- 2 tablespoon almond milk
- ½ teaspoon vanilla extract
- 1 cup semisweet chocolate chips

Directions:

1. At 350 degrees F, preheat your air fryer.
2. Mix flour with salt and baking soda in a mixing bowl.
3. Stir in vanilla extract, milk, brown sugar, sugar and butter, then mix well.
4. Fold in chocolate chips and mix evenly.
5. Grease a 7 inches round pan with oil.
6. Spread the cookie batter in the pan and place it in the air fryer basket.
7. Air fryer the cookie dough for 15 minutes.
8. Serve.

Nutritional Value (Amount per Serving):

Calories 333; Fat 15.4g; Cholesterol 0mg; Carbohydrate 46.6g; Sugars 29.3g; Protein 4.3g

Preparation Time: 15 minutes

Cooking Time: 10 minutes

Serve: 2

Ingredients:

- 2 yellow peaches
- 1/4 cup graham cracker crumbs
- 1/4 cup brown sugar
- 1/4 cup almond butter

Directions:

1. Cut the peaches into wedges.
2. Layer the air fryer basket with a baking or parchment paper.
3. Spread peaches in the prepared basket.
4. At 350 degrees F, preheat your air fryer.
5. Air fry the peaches for 5 minutes.
6. Add butter, sugar and crumbs on top of the peaches.
7. Continue air frying for 5 minutes.
8. Serve.

Nutritional Value (Amount per Serving):

Calories 187; Fat 2.5g; Cholesterol 0mg; Carbohydrate 40.8g; Sugars 33.7g; Protein 2.5g

CHERRY HAND PIES

Preparation Time: 15 minutes

Cooking Time: 15 minutes

Serve: 6-8

Ingredients:

- 1 (2-count package) refrigerated pie crusts
- 1 (21-ounce) can cherry pie filling
- 2¼ cups confectioners' sugar
- 1/4 cup almond milk

Directions:

1. At 370 degrees F, preheat your air fryer.
2. Roll out the pie crusts and cut 4-inch circles out of this dough using a cookie cutter.
3. Add a tablespoon of pie at the center of the dough circles.
4. Fold them in half and press the edges with a fork to seal.
5. Brush the hand pies with almond milk and drizzle sugar on top.
6. Place the cherry hand pies in the air fryer basket and air fry for 15 minutes.
7. Flip the hand pies once cooked halfway through.
8. Serve.

Nutritional Value (Amount per Serving):

Calories 248; Fat 10.5g; Cholesterol 0mg; Carbohydrate 37.2g; Sugars 19.9g; Protein 1.4g

APPLE PIE ROLL

Preparation Time: 10 minutes

Cooking Time: 8 minutes

Serve: 4

Ingredients:

- 21 ounce can apple pie filling
- 1/2 teaspoon lemon juice
- 1/4 teaspoon apple pie spice
- 1/8 teaspoon ground cinnamon
- 1 tablespoon all-purpose flour
- 4 roll wrappers

Directions:

1. Mix apple pie filling with lemon juice, apple pie spice, cinnamon and flour in a bowl.
2. Spread a roll wrapper on the working surface in a diamond shape position.
3. Add ¼ of the apple pie filling on one corner of the wrapper.
4. Fold the top and bottom of the wrapper and roll it neatly.
5. Wet the edges and press to seal the roll.
6. Place the rolls in the air fryer basket and spray with cooking spray.
7. At 400 degrees F, preheat your air fryer.
8. Air fry the apple pie rolls for 8 minutes in the preheated air fryer.
9. Serve.

Nutritional Value (Amount per Serving):

Calories 156; Fat 0.6g; Cholesterol 0mg; Carbohydrate 34.5g; Sugars 3.6g; Protein 5.2g

CHAPTER 7:

SEASONINGS, SAUCES, AND STAPLES

SPINACH DIP

Preparation Time: 10 minutes

Cooking Time: 30 minutes

Serve: 8

Ingredients:

- 8 oz. vegan cream cheese, softened
- 1 cup packed frozen spinach, thawed
- 1 cup grated vegan parmesan cheese
- 1 cup vegan mayonnaise
- 1/3 cup chopped water chestnuts, drained
- 1/2 cup minced onion
- 1/4 teaspoon garlic powder
- 1 teaspoon black pepper

Directions:

1. At 370 degrees F, preheat your air fryer.
2. Grease a baking dish suitable to fit the air fryer basket with oil.
3. Mix vegan cream cheese with spinach, parmesan cheese, mayonnaise, water chestnut, onion, garlic powder and black pepper in a bowl.
4. Spread this spinach mixture in the baking dish.
5. Transfer the baking dish to the air fryer basket, then air fry for 20 minutes.
6. Stir the dip and continue air frying for 10 minutes.
7. Serve.

Nutritional Value (Amount per Serving):

Calories 237; Fat 22.4g; Cholesterol 3mg; Carbohydrate 6.1g; Sugars 0.5g; Protein 3.2g

Preparation Time: 15 minutes

Cooking Time: 10 minutes

Serve: 8

Ingredients:

- 2 tablespoons olive oil
- 2 cloves garlic, minced
- 10 ounces fresh spinach
- ¼ teaspoon red pepper flakes
- 1 (14 oz) can artichoke hearts, chopped
- 4 ounces vegan cream cheese
- 4 ounces vegan mozzarella, shredded
- ½ cup vegan mayonnaise
- ½ cup coconut cream
- ¼ cup vegan Parmesan cheese, grated
- 2 splashes of hot sauce

Directions:

1. At 320 degrees F, preheat your air fryer.
2. Mix garlic oil and the rest of the ingredients in a bowl.
3. Spread this mixture in a greased pan suitable to fit the air fryer basket.
4. Place the baking pan in the air fryer basket.
5. Air fry the dip for 10 minutes in the air fryer.
6. Serve.

Nutritional Value (Amount per Serving):

Calories 237; Fat 18.6g; Cholesterol 1mg; Carbohydrate 15.6g; Sugars 1.2g; Protein 4.5g

Preparation Time: 15 minutes

Cooking Time: 25 minutes

Serve: 8

Ingredients:

- 1 (8 oz) package seitan Bacon, cooked and chopped
- 8 ounces vegan cream cheese
- 1/2 cup coconut cream
- 1/2 cup vegan mayonnaise
- 4 dashes of hot sauce
- 1/4 cup fresh parsley, chopped
- 1 clove garlic, minced
- 2 cups vegan cheddar cheese, shredded

Directions:

1. At 375 degrees F, preheat your air fryer.
2. Mix vegan cream cheese, mayonnaise and the rest of the ingredients in a bowl.
3. Spread this dip in a baking pan, suitable to fit the air fryer basket.
4. Air fry this dip for 25 minutes until bubbly.
5. Serve.

Nutritional Value (Amount per Serving):

Calories 294; Fat 18.9g; Cholesterol 0mg; Carbohydrate 4.6g; Sugars 0.5g; Protein 22.7g

Preparation Time: 15 minutes

Cooking Time: 20 minutes

Serve: 6

Ingredients:

- 1 medium eggplant, halved lengthwise
- ½ teaspoon kosher salt
- 5 ½ tablespoons olive oil
- 1 bulb garlic, peeled
- ¼ cup tahini
- 2 tablespoons lemon juice
- ¼ teaspoon ground cumin
- ⅛ teaspoon smoked paprika
- 2 tablespoons vegan feta cheese, crumbled
- 1 tablespoon fresh parsley, chopped
- ½ teaspoon lemon zest

Directions:

1. Place the eggplant in a colander and drizzle salt on top.
2. Leave the eggplant for 30 minutes, then pat it dry.
3. At 400 degrees F, preheat your air fryer.
4. Brush the eggplant with olive oil and place it in the air fryer basket.
5. Rub garlic cloves with oil and place in the basket.
6. Air fry the veggies for 20 minutes, then allow the veggies to cool.
7. Peel the veggies and blend them with the rest of the ingredients in a food processor.
8. Serve.

Nutritional Value (Amount per Serving):

Calories 180; Fat 17.3g; Cholesterol 0mg; Carbohydrate 6.8g; Sugars 2.5g; Protein 2.5g

PASTA SAUCE

Preparation Time: 15 minutes

Cooking Time: 18 minutes

Serve: 4

Ingredients:

- 1 ½ lb. tomatoes
- 1 teaspoon dried oregano
- 1/2 teaspoon ground allspice
- 2 green onions, sliced
- Salt, to taste
- 1/2 teaspoon balsamic vinegar
- 1 teaspoon maple syrup

Directions:

1. At 375 degrees F, preheat your air fryer.
2. Add tomatoes to a baking pan, suitable to fit the air fryer basket.
3. Drizzle oregano, allspice, salt and vinegar over the tomatoes.
4. Place the prepared tomato's pan in the air fryer basket and air fry for 18 minutes.
5. Puree the cooked tomatoes mixture with the rest of the ingredients.
6. Serve.

Nutritional Value (Amount per Serving):

Calories 39; Fat 0.4g; Cholesterol 0mg; Carbohydrate 8.7g; Sugars 5.7g; Protein 1.7g

Preparation Time: 15 minutes

Cooking Time: 25 minutes

Serve: 8

Ingredients:

- 2 (16 ounces) cans of refried beans
- 1 (8 ounces) package vegan cream cheese
- 1 cup coconut cream
- 1 taco seasoning packet
- 2 cups vegan mozzarella cheese, shredded
- 2 cups vegan cheddar cheese, shredded

Directions:

1. At 350 degrees F, preheat your air fryer.
2. Blend beans with cream cheese and the rest of the ingredients in a food processor for 1 minute.
3. Spread this bean mixture in a baking pan, suitable to fit the air fryer basket.
4. Air fry the beans dip for 25 minutes until bubbly.
5. Serve.

Nutritional Value (Amount per Serving):

Calories 258; Fat 16.5g; Cholesterol 22mg; Carbohydrate 19.8g; Sugars 0.3g; Protein 8.1g

Preparation Time: 15 minutes

Cooking Time: 25 minutes

Serve: 8

Ingredients:

- 8 ounces vegan cream cheese
- 1 cup vegan mayonnaise
- 1 cup vegan Parmesan cheese, shredded
- 1 cup diced sweet onion
- 2 teaspoon black pepper

Directions:

1. At 350 degrees F, preheat your Air fryer.
2. Mix vegan cream cheese, mayonnaise, cheese, onion and black pepper in a bowl.
3. Spread this mixture in a baking pan, suitable to fit the air fryer basket.
4. Air fry this dip for 25 minutes in the air fryer until golden brown.
5. Serve.

Nutritional Value (Amount per Serving):

Calories 208; Fat 18.8g; Cholesterol 7mg; Carbohydrate 5g; Sugars 0.6g; Protein 5g

Preparation Time: 15 minutes

Cooking Time: 15 minutes

Serve: 8

Ingredients:

- 1 cup coconut cream
- 1/2 teaspoon mustard powder
- 1 teaspoon garlic powder
- 1 teaspoon dried thyme
- 1 teaspoon herbs of Provence
- 8 ounces vegan mozzarella cheese, shredded
- 8 ounces vegan cheddar cheese, shredded
- 1 cup basil leaves chopped
- 1 cup diced tomatoes
- Extra basil leaves

Directions:

1. At 350 degrees F, preheat your air fryer.
2. Mix cream with thyme, herbs, mustard powder, basil and cheese in a bowl.
3. Spread this mixture in a baking dish suitable to fit the air fryer.
4. Top the dip mixture with tomatoes and air fry for 15 minutes.
5. Serve.

Nutritional Value (Amount per Serving):

Calories 157; Fat 13.3g; Cholesterol 0mg; Carbohydrate 9g; Sugars 1.7g; Protein 1g

Preparation Time: 10 minutes

Cooking Time: 11 minutes

Serve: 6

Ingredients:

- 2 red bell peppers, halved
- 12 large garlic cloves
- 1 1/2 cups boiled chickpeas
- 3 tablespoons tahini
- 2 tablespoons lemon juice
- 3 tablespoons olive oil
- 2 teaspoon red chilli powder
- 1/2 teaspoon salt
- 1 tablespoon water

Directions:

1. At 370 degrees F, preheat your air fryer.
2. Remove the seeds and stems of the bell peppers.
3. Toss the peppers and garlic with oil in the air fryer basket and air fry for 7 minutes.
4. Stir the peppers and continue air frying for 4 minutes.
5. Transfer the peppers to a bowl, cover with plastic wrap and leave for 15 minutes.
6. Remove the charred skin and cut it into strips.
7. Puree the peppers, garlic, chickpeas and rest of the ingredients in a blender for 1 minute.
8. Serve.

Nutritional Value (Amount per Serving):

Calories 187; Fat 8.6g; Cholesterol 0mg; Carbohydrate 22.5g; Sugars 4.6g; Protein 7.1g

Preparation Time: 10 minutes

Cooking Time: 15 minutes

Serve: 4

Ingredients:

- 3 Roma tomatoes, quartered
- 1 yellow onion, peeled and quartered
- 1 jalapeño
- 1 tablespoon cilantro
- 1 tablespoon garlic, peeled

Directions:

1. At 385 degrees F, preheat your air fryer.
2. Toss tomatoes with onion, jalapeno, cilantro and garlic in a bowl.
3. Spread the veggies in a baking pan, suitable to fit the air fryer basket.
4. Air fry the tomato mixture for 15 minutes.
5. Puree this tomato mixture in a blender.
6. Serve.

Nutritional Value (Amount per Serving):

Calories 32; Fat 0.2g; Cholesterol 0mg; Carbohydrate 7.1g; Sugars 3.7g; Protein 1.3g

CONCLUSION

Well, it's about time that you plug in that powerful air frying appliance of yours and get started with your plant-based cooking. Since this cookbook offers a number of recipes in each section, you can pick and choose any to create an entire menu of your own. There are recipes for breakfast, salads, snacks, main dishes, desserts and sauce etc., so that you could easily select a delicious meal of your choice, air fry it in your own kitchen and enjoy!

Printed in Great Britain
by Amazon

15872202R00061